TimeLine™

LOONY A AT MEDIEVAL

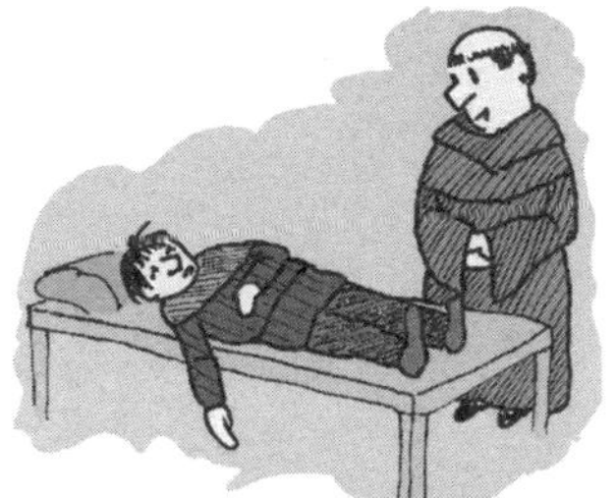

THE BOTTOM LINE FACTS OF HISTORY - WITH A COMIC TWIST

words & pictures© Peeby

A Loony Look at Medieval Life

Published by Timeline.co.uk The Chapel, Belgrave Road, Dover, Kent, CT17 9QY, England

First published 2004 by Timeline.co.uk

A CIP catalogue record for this book is available from the British Library

ISBN 0-9547242-1-6

Printed and bound in Great Britain

Introduction

MEDIEVAL LIFE
(1066-1485)

History suggests that the past was not a whole heap of fun. Seems it was all wars and warlords intent on battles, beheadings and bumpings-off. And you're expected to remember the dates of who did what to whom.

But have a look at what medieval life might have been like - if Peeby had been there to see the comic side.

And after you've enjoyed the joke the bottom line will give you the facts. It will entertain you and maybe even surprise you; proof that our fiction is funnier than fact!

FACT: THE NORMANS (1066-1154) IMPROVED ARCHITECTURE, CULTURE, ORGANISATION AND GOVERNMENT. THEY ESTABLISHED THE 'ENGLISH TONGUE'. SOCIAL LIFE WAS 'FEUDAL'.

I TOLD YOU THESE SUMMER PILGRIMAGES ARE NOTHING BUT TRAFFIC JAMS.

OK, I'LL TRY THIS SIDE RUT.

Peeby

FACT: DURING THE MIDDLE AGES, WATLING STREET, ERMINE STREET, FOSSE WAY AND ICKNIELD STREET WERE REGARDED AS ROYAL ROADS.

FACT: DOMESDAY CENSUS, 1086. THE LORD OF THE MANOR (BARON) OWNED ALL THE LAND. VILLAGERS FARMED SOME OF IT IN RETURN FOR WORKING FOR HIM.

FACT: KING HENRY I (r.1100-35) DECREED THAT ONE YARD BE THE DISTANCE FROM HIS NOSE TO AN OUTSTRETCHED THUMB.

FACT: DURING THE MIDDLE AGES PIGEONS WERE THE CHIEF SOURCE OF FRESH MEAT IN BRITAIN.

FACT: THE ANGEVIN PERIOD (1154-1272) SAW CIVIL & RELIGIOUS POWER STRUGGLES. REFORMED POLITICAL & JUDICIAL SYSTEMS & ESTABLISHED NATIONAL LIBERTIES.

FACT: BECKET MURDERED IN 1170 WAS CANONIZED IN 1173. PILGRIMAGES TO CANTERBURY FEATURED IN CHAUCER'S BOOK, CANTERBURY TALES.

FACT: TOURNAMENTS GREW SO POPULAR, HENRY II FORBADE THE SPORT. RICHARD I RELAXED THE ORDER AND LATER IN 1299 ROYAL LICENCES WERE REQUIRED.

FACT: MOST PEOPLE DIED BEFORE THEY WERE FIFTY. DOCTORS BELIEVED THAT ILLNESS WAS CAUSED BY 'BAD' BLOOD, OFTEN CUTTING THE VEIN TO RELEASE IT.

FACT: KING JOHN FOSTERED THE BREED OF THE OLD ENGLISH GREAT (BLACK) HORSE, VALUED FOR ITS ABILITY TO CARRY THE WEIGHT OF THE ARMOURED KNIGHT.

YOU'RE LEARNING TO BE A FARMER?

YES, I TAKE MY HAY-LEVELS NEXT WEEK.

FACT: VILLAGERS COULDN'T LEAVE THE LAND WITHOUT THE BARON'S PERMISSION.

FACT: (FRIAR) ROGER BACON, KNOWN AS DOCTOR MIRABILIS (c.1220-92) WAS ASSOCIATED WITH GUNPOWDER (1249), THE MAGNIFYING GLASS (1266) AND MUCH ELSE SCIENTIFIC.

AT THE LAST FAIR - YOU WENT ON A 'WINE DIET'. WHAT DID YOU LOSE?

OH...ABOUT A WEEK!

Peeby

FACT: FAIRS, HELD ONCE A YEAR, LASTED SEVERAL DAYS. EUROPEAN MERCHANTS CAME TO SELL WINES, SILKS, FURS AND WEAPONS.

FACT: PEOPLE TRAVELLING ON 'ROYAL ROADS' WERE CONSIDERED UNDER THE KING'S PROTECTION. ANY ATTACKERS WERE LIABLE TO A FINE OF ONE HUNDRED SHILLINGS.

FACT: ON A FEAST DAY, A BARON'S BANQUET IN THE GREAT HALL OF THE MANOR COULD LAST FIVE HOURS AND CONSIST OF UP TO 40 DISHES.

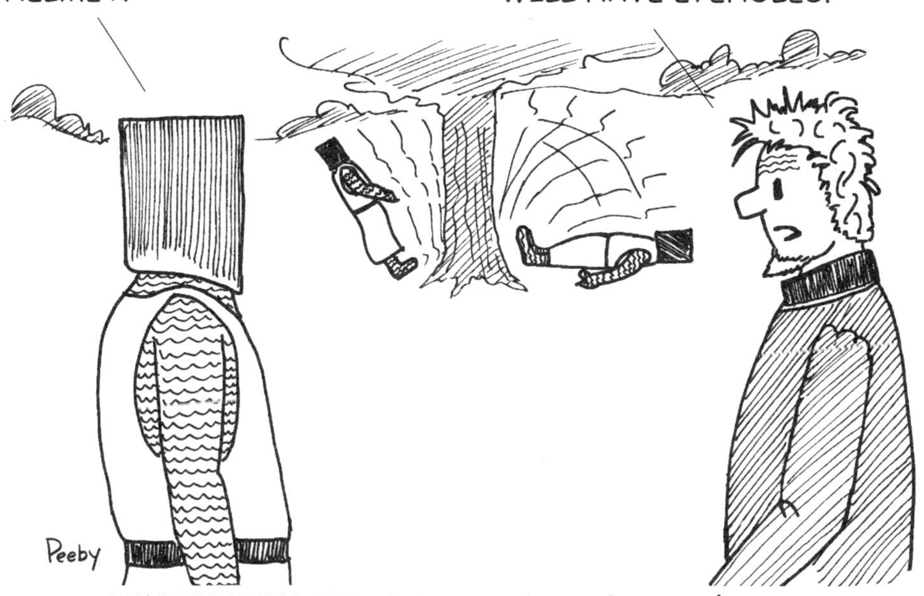

FACT: BEFORE THE INTRODUCTION OF PLATE ARMOUR, 13th. CENTURY KNIGHTS HAD A HAUBERK: A COAT OF MAIL WITH A HOOD UNDER THE CLOSE-FITTING HELMET.

FACT: RELIGION WAS IMPORTANT IN THE MIDDLE AGES, EVERYONE GOING TO CHURCH SEVERAL TIMES A WEEK. THE CHURCH BECAME RICH AND POWERFUL.

FACT: PEOPLE IN THE TOWNS COPIED THE STYLES OF THE RICH. THEY USED CHEAPER MATERIALS.

FACT: PHYSICIANS USED ASTROLOGICAL CHARTS PLUS HERBS, SPELLS AND CHARMS. MOST CURES WERE USELESS.

YOU CAN'T SAY THAT HALF OF THEM ARE CROOKS!

LET'S PUT IT THIS WAY - HALF OF THEM ARE **NOT** CROOKS.

Peeby

FACT: THE LATER PLANTAGENET PERIOD (1272-1485) WAS ONE OF GENERAL EXPANSION: LAWS, TRADE AND COMMERCE AND WITH IT THE RISE OF THE MIDDLE CLASSES.

FACT: PEASANTS' MAIN FOOD WAS BREAD. SOME KEPT CHICKENS, PIGS AND COWS FOR THE EGGS, BACON AND MILK. THE ANIMALS GRAZED ON COMMON LAND.

FACT: TOWNS WERE SMALL IN THE MIDDLE AGES. LARGEST CITY IN 1300 WAS LONDON WITH 60,000 OUT OF A 3 TO 6 MILLION POPULATION.

FACT: PARENTS PAID MASTER CRAFTSMEN TO TRAIN THEIR CHILDREN AS APPRENTICES. HE WOULD SLEEP IN THE WORKSHOP AND WAS PAID NOTHING.

FACT: THE BLACK DEATH PLAGUE, 1348 KILLED ONE THIRD OF THE POPULATION WITHIN TWO YEARS. A DOCTOR'S PROTECTIVE OUTFIT HAD HERBS IN THE BEAK TO FILTER AIR.

FACT: CARRIAGES WERE NOT VERY COMFORTABLE. RICH PEOPLE USUALLY TRAVELLED ON HORSEBACK.

FACT: THE INVENTION OF GUNS, THEN CANNONS CHANGED THE WAY BATTLES WERE FOUGHT. CASTLES, NOW MORE VULNERABLE MEANT THAT FEWER WERE BUILT AFTER 1350.

FACT: THERE WERE NO RULES TO FOOTBALL. SOME PLAYERS WERE HURT, EVEN KILLED. KING EDWARD III BANNED IT BECAUSE IT CONFLICTED WITH ARCHERY PRACTICE.

FACT: AFTER THE BLACK DEATH, SURVIVING, OVERWORKED PEASANTS WANTED WAGES AND FREEDOM. THE STATUTE OF LABOURERS, 1351 STOPPED IT AND ANGERED THEM.

FACT: DURING THE LORD OF THE MANOR'S BANQUET, MINSTRELS SANG AND PLAYED IN THE GALLERY WHILE JESTERS, TUMBLERS AND ACROBATS ENTERTAINED.

THE SET FOR 50 PENCE.
HALF A SET FOR 30 PENCE.

OK. I'LL HAVE THE OTHER
HALF A SET FOR 20 PENCE!

FACT: GUILDS WERE CLUBS STARTED BY MASTER CRAFTSMEN. EACH TRADE HAVING ITS OWN GUILD. ONLY MEMBERS WERE ALLOWED TO MAKE AND SELL THE GOODS.

FACT: JOHN WYCLIFFE (c.1330-84), RELIGIOUS REFORMER, ISSUED THE FIRST ENGLISH TRANSLATION OF THE BIBLE, 1380. HIS FOLLOWERS WERE 'LOLLARDS'.

FACT: A WEALTHY FAMILY'S SON COULD TRAIN TEN YEARS TO BE A KNIGHT, FIRST AS A PAGE, THEN A SQUIRE. HE DRESSED THE KNIGHT FOR BATTLE.

FACT: PEOPLE CAME TO FAIRS FROM FAR AFIELD. TO HEAR THE NEWS, TO DANCE, WATCH JUGGLERS, CLOWNS AND PERFORMING ANIMALS.

FACT: MONASTERIES WHERE MONKS WORKED AND PRAYED BECAME RICH THROUGH THE WOOL TRADE.

FACT: UNTIL THE 16th. CENTURY, THE RICH WERE BURIED INSIDE CHURCHES AND PAUPERS OUTSIDE.

THEY HATE THE WINTER...

YES, THE COLD GOES RIGHT THROUGH THEM!

Peeby

FACT: DURING THE MIDDLE AGES, CORPSES WERE OFTEN BOILED TO REMOVE THE FLESH SO THEY COULD BE TRANSPORTED MORE EASILY.

FACT: A FOOTBALL WAS A PIG'S BLADDER FILLED WITH PEAS. MEN FROM OPPOSING VILLAGES WOULD ATTEMPT TO REACH THE OTHER'S MARKET CROSS WITH IT.

WHAT'S THAT COW DOING, EATING MY GRASS?

IT'S ALL RIGHT SIRE. HE'S A LAWNMOOER.

FACT: VILLAGERS GATHERED WOOD, NUTS AND BERRIES FROM THE FOREST. THEIR ANIMALS GRAZED ON SHARED COMMON LAND.

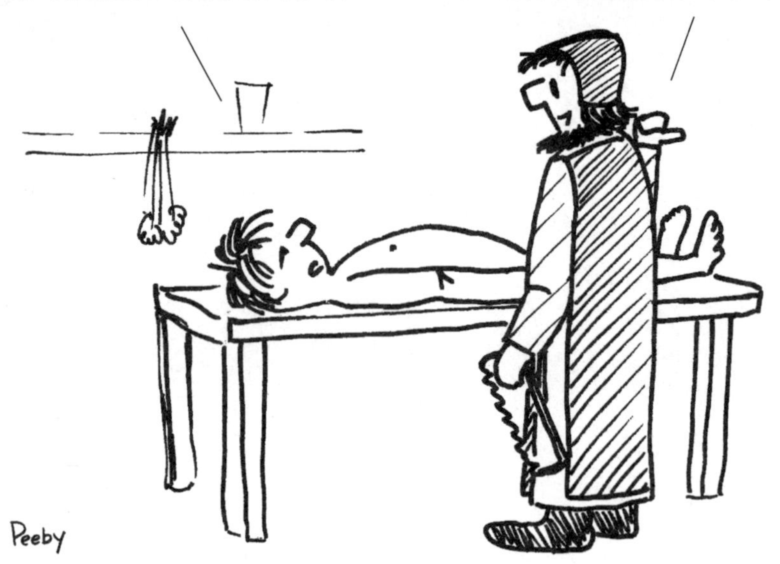

FACT: SURGEONS WERE BARBERS WHO PULLED TEETH AND DID SMALL OPERATIONS. RED AND WHITE STRIPED BARBER'S POLE DEPICTED BLOOD AND BANDAGES OF THE TRADE.

FACT: WHEN A POLL TAX (1381) ADDED TO THE PEASANTS' WOES, JOHN BALL A POOR PRIEST CONVINCED THEM TO MARCH FOR FREEDOM AND HIGHER WAGES.

FACT: THE REEVE WAS APPOINTED BY THE BAILIFF, OR ELECTED BY THE VILLAGERS AND SHARED OUT THE JOBS IN THE VILLAGE.

FACT: WAT TYLER WAS ELECTED LEADER OF THE 1381 'PEASANTS' REVOLT'. THEY MET THE KING BUT WAT TYLER WAS KILLED BY THE LORD MAYOR OF LONDON.

FACT: AN APPRENTICE COULDN'T GET MARRIED OR EVEN GO TO INNS. AFTER SEVEN YEARS TRAINING HE WOULD BRECOME A JOURNEYMAN AND GET HIS FIRST PAY.

FACT: NORMAL TRAVELLERS WERE GOVERNMENT OFFICIALS AND NOBLES ON THE KING'S BUSINESS, MERCHANTS BUYING AND SELLING GOODS AND SOLDIERS, OFF TO WAR.

FACT: GEOFFREY CHAUCER (1345-1400) WROTE THE CANTERBURY TALES IN THE 1380s. IN 1394, RICHARD II GRANTED HIM A PENSION OF £20 PER YEAR FOR LIFE.

FACT: PILGRIMS WANTING FORGIVENESS WENT TO PRAY AT A SHRINE. FROM NEARBY STALLS THEY WOULD BUY RELICS, HOLY WATER AND PIECES OF SAINTS' CLOTHING.

FACT: AT BANQUETS, RICH PEOPLE SAT 'ABOVE' THE SALT, POOR PEOPLE 'BELOW'.

FACT: AGINCOURT 1415, WAS ONE BATTLE IN THE HUNDRED YEARS WAR (1357-1453) AGAINST THE FRENCH. LONGBOWMEN FIRED UP TO TWELVE ARROWS A MINUTE.

FACT: 15th. CENTURY LAW FORBADE ALL BUT NOBILITY TO CARRY HANDKERCHIEFS.

FACT: FIRE WAS A GREAT DANGER IN TOWNS BECAUSE OF WOODEN HOUSES AND WORKSHOPS CROWDED TOGETHER.

FACT: AFTER SEVERAL YEARS AN APPRENTICE WOULD PRODUCE A 'MASTERPIECE' AND IF IT WAS GOOD HE'D BE ENTERED INTO THE GUILD AND HAVE HIS OWN SHOP.

FACT: 15th. CENTURY FASHION FOR SQUARE-ENDED SHOES WAS STARTED BY THE FRENCH KING CHARLES VIII WHO HAD SIX TOES ON ONE FOOT.

I THINK I'M GOING INSANE, BROTHER BRIAN.

I KNOW HOW YOU FEEL. ISN'T IT MADDENING?

Peeby

FACT: MONASTERIES GAVE MONEY AND FOOD TO THE NEEDY. TRAVELLERS COULD STAY FREE FOR TWO NIGHTS. THEY WERE HOSPITALS FOR THE POOR.

FACT: MEDIEVAL SPORTS INCLUDED FIGHTING, WRESTLING, SHIN KICKING, QUARTER STAFFS, ARCHERY, SKITTLES AND STOOLBALL.

FACT: FASHIONS FOR THE WEALTHY CHANGED A GREAT DEAL DURING THE MIDDLE AGES. PEOPLE WERE RICHER AND SO BOUGHT BETTER, MORE DECORATIVE CLOTHES.

THAT DOG BIT YOUR LEG! DID YOU PUT ANYTHING ON IT?

NO, HE SEEMED TO LIKE IT, THE WAY IT WAS.

FACT: IN TOWNS, STREETS WERE NARROW, DIRTY AND SMELLY. ALSO, PEOPLE THREW OUT RUBBISH WHICH ATTRACTED RATS AND FLIES.

FACT: BARONS OWNED VAST AREAS OF LAND ON WHICH THEY BUILT CASTLES. THEY PROTECTED IT WITH THEIR OWN SOLDIERS.

FACT: WILLIAM CAXTON PRINTED HIS FIRST BOOK IN ENGLAND IN 1477. BY THE TIME HE DIED IN 1491 HE HAD PRINTED NEARLY ONE HUNDRED TITLES.

FACT: PEASANTS LIVED IN THATCH-ROOFED WOODEN HUTS, THEY AT ONE END, THE ANIMALS IN THE OTHER. IT WAS DIRTY, SMELLY AND DARK.

FACT: BY 1485, PEOPLE DIDN'T THINK THAT MONASTERIES WERE IMPORTANT. FRIARS WHO TRAVELLED WERE POPULAR. PERHAPS BISHOPS WERE NOT...

LOOK OUT FOR OTHER

LOONY LOOK BOOKS:

KINGS & QUEENS

ROMAN BRITAIN

THE VIKINGS

CELTIC TIMES

THE TUDORS